APR 1 1

Super Sized!

African Elephant

The World's Biggest Land Mammal

by Kirsten Hall

Consultant: Caitlin O'Connell-Rodwell
Research Associate
Leland Stanford Junior University
Stanford, CA

BEARPORT
PUBLISHING

New York, New York

Credits

Cover, ©SouWest Photography/Shutterstock; 2–3, ©Tom Brakefield/Creatas; 4, Kathrin Ayer; 4–5, ©Digital Vision; 6, ©Digital Vision; 7BKG, ©Digital Vision; 8, ©Tom Brakefield/Creatas; 9, ©Ablestock; 10, ©AGE Fotostock; 11, ©Corbis; 12 (inset), ©Tom Brakefield/Creatas; 12–13, ©Digital Vision; 14 (inset), ©Ablestock; 14–15, ©Tom Brakefield/Creatas; 16–17, ©Ablestock; 18, ©Corbis; 19, ©Corbis; 20–21, ©Tom Brakefield/Creatas; 22L, ©Ablestock; 22C, ©Photodisc Images; 22R, ©Digital Vision; 23TL, ©Digital Vision; 23TR, ©Tom Brakefield/Creatas; 23BL, ©Ablestock 23BR, ©Tom Brakefield/Creatas; 23BKG, ©Tom Brakefield/Creatas.

Publisher: Kenn Goin
Senior Editor: Lisa Wiseman
Editorial Development: Nancy Hall, Inc.
Creative Director: Spencer Brinker
Photo Researcher: Carousel Research, Inc.: Mary Teresa Giancoli
Design: Otto Carbajal

Library of Congress Cataloging-in-Publication Data

Hall, Kirsten.
 African elephant : the world's biggest land mammal / by Kirsten Hall.
    p. cm. — (SuperSized!)
 Includes bibliographical references and index.
 ISBN-13: 978-1-59716-387-3 (library binding)
 ISBN-10: 1-59716-387-2 (library binding)
 1. African elephant—Juvenile literature. I. Title.

QL737.P98H3433 2007
599.67'4—dc22

                                        2006035294

For more information, write to Bearport Publishing Company, Inc., 101 Fifth Avenue, Suite 6R, New York, New York 10003. Printed in the United States of America in North Mankato, Minnesota.

082010
080910CGC

10 9 8 7 6 5 4

Contents

Biggest on Land

The African elephant is the biggest animal that lives on land.

A male African elephant weighs about as much as three white rhinoceroses.

An African elephant can grow up to 13 feet (3.9 m) tall. It can weigh more than 6 tons (5.4 metric tons).

Many Kinds of Homes

African elephants are found in Africa.

They live in **grasslands**, forests, and near rivers.

Elephants can go a long time without water.

So they are able to live in dry places, too.

There are two kinds of elephants—African and Asian. Asian elephants are smaller than African elephants.

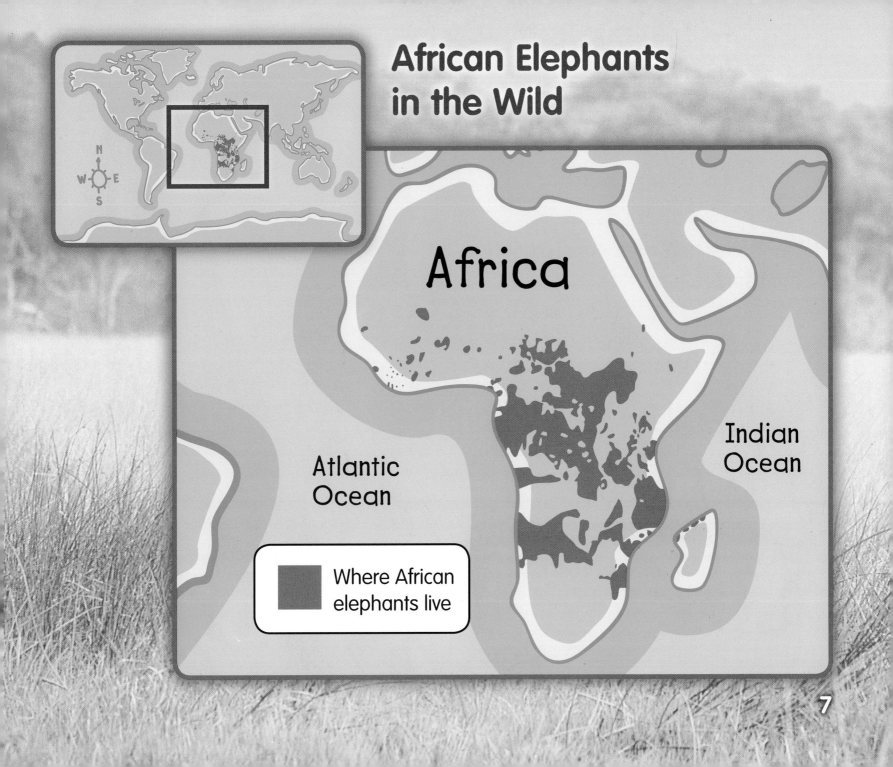

African Elephants in the Wild

Africa

Atlantic Ocean

Indian Ocean

N W E S

Where African elephants live

Flapping Ears

An African elephant has very large ears.

Elephants flap their ears to cool themselves.

Africa

An African elephant's ear is shaped like the land of Africa.

Inside Teeth

An African elephant has four teeth inside its mouth.

Each tooth weighs more than a brick.

The elephant uses its teeth to chew food.

It eats grasses, leaves, fruits, and bark.

An elephant lives about 70 years. It dies when its teeth wear out and it can no longer chew food.

tooth

Outside Teeth

An African elephant also has two front teeth called **tusks**.

They grow outside its mouth.

Elephants use their tusks to dig up plants.

Sometimes elephants fight each other with their tusks.

An elephant's tusks never stop growing. The largest are about 8 feet (2.4 m) long and can weigh up to 130 pounds (59 kg).

tusks

13

Trunks at Work

Elephants use their **trunks** to do many things.

They suck in water through their trunks and spray it into their mouths.

They can even grab things with them.

An African elephant's trunk can be 7 feet (2 m) long. It can weigh up to 300 pounds (136 kg).

trunk

Group Living

Adult female African elephants live in groups of about ten.

Young male and female elephants live with the group, too.

One adult female is in charge of each group.

She is usually the oldest and largest elephant.

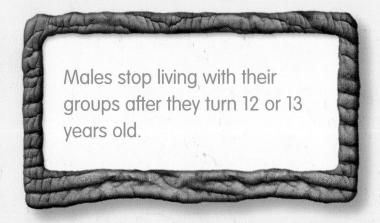

Males stop living with their groups after they turn 12 or 13 years old.

One Big Baby

A mother elephant gives birth to one baby at a time.

The big baby can weigh as much as 250 pounds (113 kg).

It is cared for by its mother, aunts, and older sisters.

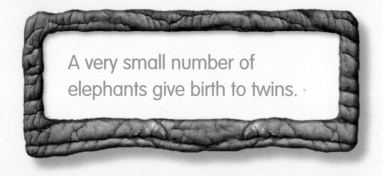

A very small number of elephants give birth to twins.

baby elephant

Big Trouble

African elephants are in danger.

People use their land to build homes and grow food.

Hunters kill them for their **ivory** tusks.

Today there are laws to help keep these giant animals safe.

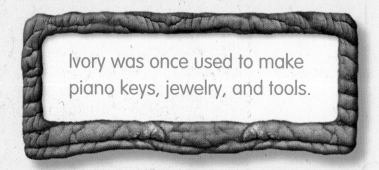

Ivory was once used to make piano keys, jewelry, and tools.

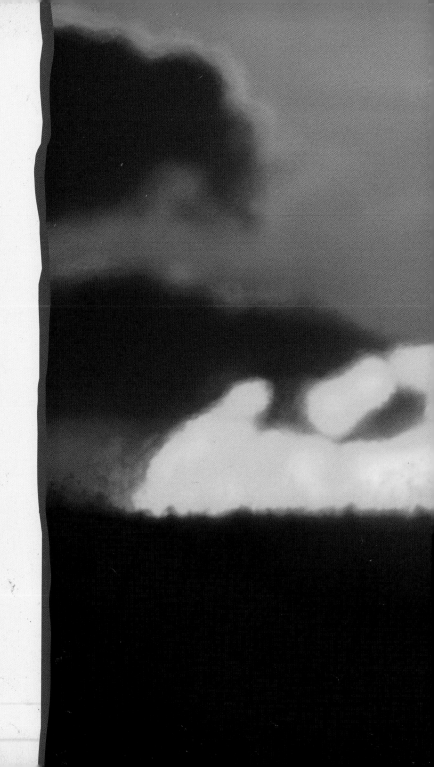

More Big Mammals

African elephants belong to a group of animals called mammals. Almost all mammals give birth to live young. The babies drink milk from their mothers. Mammals are also warm-blooded and have hair or fur on their skin.

Here are three more big land mammals.

White Rhinoceros

The white rhinoceros is the second biggest land mammal. It can grow to 7 feet (2.1 m) tall and weigh up to 2 tons (1.8 metric tons).

Water Buffalo

The water buffalo can grow to be 6 feet (1.8 m) tall. It can weigh up to 1 ton (0.9 metric ton).

Hippopotamus

The hippopotamus can grow to about 5 feet (1.5 m) tall. It can weigh up to 3.5 tons (3.1 metric tons).

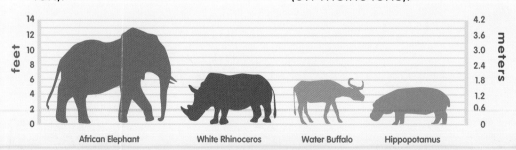

Glossary

grasslands
(GRASS-landz)
large, open areas
of land where
grass grows

trunks
(TRUHNGKS)
elephants' long
noses

ivory (EYE-vur-ee)
a hard white
material that
forms the tusks
of elephants and
certain other
animals

tusks (TUHSKS)
long, curved,
pointed teeth
that grow outside
the mouths of
elephants and
other animals

Index

Read More

Eckart, Edana. *African Elephant.* Danbury, CT: Children's Press (2003).

Hall, Margaret. *Elephants and Their Calves.* Mankato, MN: Capstone Press (2003).

Johnston, Marianne. *Elephants.* New York: PowerKids Press (1998).

Learn More Online

To learn more about African elephants, visit **www.bearportpublishing.com/SuperSized**